Az együttöltött szép évek
emlékére, sok-sok, igaz
szeretettel Juszit és Örs
Bp. 98. okt. 23.

HUNGARY
In the Heart of Europe

HUNG

Péter Korniss

Officina Nova

ARY In the Heart of Europe

Preface by Árpád Göncz • Introduction by István Nemeskürty

Can a camera lens be objective?

It must be, as it captures only what it sees.

Can a camera lens be partial and subjective?

It must be, as it captures what its owner aims it at.

And the photographer is an artist: he has an established view of the world. An internal view that he wants to confirm, even unconsciously, by selecting the subject of a picture.

Thus the lens is a tool for the artistic rendering of the world.

A final question: does the lens have sentiments as well? Such as affection?

Of course it has! Open this book anywhere at random, and affection radiates from it. The focused affection of a human life, an artist's life.

Affection for people. For the land that the people in the pictures call home. For our shared homeland, Hungary, and for us who, along with the artist, populate this country. The living subjects of these pictures. Youths kissing passionately or the elderly living through – struggling through – two generations. They cannot be torn from this land, which they learned to see, and which Péter Korniss learned to make others see.

Göncz Árpád

years, with water mains, a sewage system, public lighting and cobblestone streets.

The opposite of this monumental town-masterpiece is another Hungarian specialty encountered in this album: farmsteads.

In a seemingly endless field, a lonely house stands in the shadow of a few trees; its dwellers and owners are one family. This is the smallest human community. The closest neighbor family lives three kilometers away. They still visit each other; on Sundays they go to church by horse-and-cart; and the children go to school by foot throughout the school year, in spring or winter. King Saint Stephen ordained that every tenth village must erect a church and maintain it. A larger community, the village, developed around the churches, with a priest, shops, later a physician, a school and, naturally, a pub.

The isolated life on the farmsteads carries a number of disadvantages. Yet it provides a feeling of self-sufficiency, freedom and independence, more important than any modern convenience. Of course, the world of farmsteads is situated on plains; this is the world of the Great Hungarian Plains, with its cattle herds and studs.

It is noteworthy how man is positioned in the landscapes of Péter Korniss.

For the artist a plant, grass, a tree or a flower is just as organic a living being as an animal or a man. The main subject is the landscape, even if it is a town or a palace: living, acting and functioning. The herdsman and his dog, the shepherd driving his flock are part of nature. Two lonely trees on the plain, three horses meditating, and the almond tree blossoming with a provocative spite among the bare vine-sticks are just as dramatic subjects as man. Everything breathes together with nature: the woman on a bicycle in front of an inimically indifferent white wall, old women ringing the bell with a pride of the trade noted by the world; the feasting and mourning people of processions, weddings and funerals. The arches are also the companions, parts of the life of the monk walking on the corridor of a monastery; as if the people playing music in the

Baroque palace were listened to sympathetically even by the walls and the furniture. The passage encloses the one walking in it, so it is not obvious whether it is protecting him, guarding him or taking him captive. Will the child thrown high in the air above the water of Lake Balaton find his way back to his father's arms or fall into the water?

Add to this the colors, the lights and the shadows. Each of them epic and dramatic elements of the story. Because this book is also a story. It tells something about a people, a land in which they live and which they chose 1100 years ago, then transformed in their own image, either in league with the forces of nature or against them.

So this man is not only a part of the landscape but also its shaper and determining factor. Determining in the sense that he creates: a house, a church, a castle, a town. He builds.

In one of the pictures we can see a smiling old shepherd as he proudly shows his carved sticks. This is a key picture. Certainly the reader has already encountered artistic carvings – if nowhere else, then in shops in towns. But here we can still see a shepherd guarding his flock, as he carves, immersed in his work, while his dog keeps the animals in line. Every shepherd people, including the Hungarians, preferred easily movable works when setting on the road: carpets, tapestries, goldsmith's works of art and wood carvings. Genuine stories can be observed on a shepherd's stick in a ribbon-like presentation, as on the Traianus column in Rome. The carvings are not merely for decoration; they are tales, or rather Hungarian history, and the dramas of myths preceding written history bloom from them. From where do these people know history? The historical consciousness of the Hungarian population still thrives, mainly among the people of the villages. Is wood carving useful? It does not make the shepherd's stick any stronger or more useful. But it makes it beautiful and it gives joy. Only man is able to think like this. If a society forgets or ignores the aesthetics of this "superfluousness," it is doomed to wither away.

This collection of photographs also provides such joy.

The Crusader armies also made their way through Hungary. Arab and Jewish merchants sold their commodities from each of the trade centers and gave international money trade a boost. As a consequence, medieval Hungary, whose borders touched the Carpathians and stretching beyond the Sava River on the south, reached the Adriatic Sea coast, developed into one of Europe's most significant empires of the time.

This empire fell apart in the mid-16th century, partly due to the attack of the Ottoman Turks and partly to a change in the European balance of power. Following the discovery of America, the European power relationships and merchant routes changed. The coastal states (the Netherlands, England, France and Spain), acquiring the treasures of the new continents, became great powers while Hungary, situated at the geometric center of Europe, defined by a closed geographical unity until then and lying at the crossroads of the North-South and East-West merchant routes, was pushed to the edge of the known world. Even the Adriatic and Mediterranean Seas were dwarfed in comparison to the world's oceans. This is why the once huge and powerful Venetian Republic fell.

In addition, the expansionist Ottoman Empire attacked Hungary several times beginning in 1526 and in 1541 occupied the central third of the country. Hungary's western and eastern parts fell under Habsburg rule, and its developed and rich hilly southeastern section became the principality of Transylvania, controlled by the Turkish sultan but enjoying relative political independence.

At the start of the 18th century, when the Turkish occupiers were driven out of Hungary with the help of the Habsburg army and the other European states, all Hungary was forced under the Habsburg emperor's crown. The country gained some degree of internal political independence in principle rather than in practice. (The Habsburg emperors were also the crowned kings of Hungary.) A decades long movement toward national autonomy ripened into a revolution for independence in 1848. It was defeated only in the late summer of 1849 by the combined forces of two great powers, the Austrian emperor and the Russian czar.

In 1867 a compromise was reached with the Habsburg empire, and a dualist empire, the Austro-Hungarian Monarchy, was established. This lasted until 1918. Partly as a consequence of the Paris peace treaties, Hungary was detached from Austria and, although severely mutilated in its territory, began to enjoy independence, which was interrupted for 40 years after World War II.

This album includes the relics of these historical periods: the church masterpieces in the Gothic style, the Romanesque chapels, frescoes, monasteries, Renaissance mansions and Baroque palaces.

The establishment and resettlement of one of the medieval capitals of the country, Buda, deserves mention as a unique example of town planning.

The town of Buda was situated near the ruins of an ancient Roman settlement on a plain along the Danube River, around what is today the right bridgehead of Árpád Bridge. This rich and flourishing town was destroyed in a Mongol attack in 1241. As the Mongols were unable to conquer towns built on hills, King Béla IV ordered Buda rebuilt a few miles south, also on the Danube, on a rocky hill. The town, inheriting the name Buda, was designed with engineer's consciousness and expertise, as if planned with a ruler. (The old town received the name Óbuda – Old Buda.) The streets, side streets, squares, churches and monasteries in carefully planned sites can be admired even today. South of the town, a royal palace was simultaneously built onto another cliff.

The construction of the new Buda took place in an amazingly short period of time, unprecedented in the history of Europe. Even today's technology could not accomplish such a task. The town was completed by the mid-1250s, in ten

"this landscape is a map"

In our disjointed crisis-ridden age, a fine artist and his audience do not even dare to put down the words "beauty" and "joy," since you see, it "only" had to be noticed and "only" had to be photographed. And created. And "only" had to be photographed, because the picture conveys the artist's world of consciousness, launching an aesthetic and spiritual process in our consciousness as well. However, these are both preconditions for every genuine work of art.

Beyond this, the photographs of this volume are dramas at the same time; a string of dramatic events set to motion before our spiritual eyes either when a pair of deer walk through the grain field, or a strip of land cut by the green of bushes breaks the tranquil, seemingly endless continuity of the ripened seeds, or an island resists the calm but merciless strength of a river bordering it on two sides, a strength that is tamed to a vision by the silky vapor of twilight.

The country presented here to the viewer is small. Its territory is only 93,000 square kilometers, essentially a colorful patch on the multicolored tapestry of Europe – the size of Austria, its western neighbor, and twice the size of Belgium, the Netherlands or Denmark. It has 10.5 million inhabitants. Since 1946 the country has been a republic; previously it was a kingdom. Hungary's capital is Budapest, home to more than 20 percent of the country's population.

Although it has no tall mountains, Hungary is a diverse land for its size. One need only travel 50 or 60 kilometers to find a completely different world. Hills cut by hidden valleys; hills covered by dense forests, majestic even at their short height of 800 or 1000 meters; lakes popping up unexpectedly; the big lake, the Balaton, visible from a distance, was once the favorite holiday resort for the rich in the one-time Roman Empire; pusztas [plains]: rich pastures interspersed with orchards, littered with puddles; volcanic hills producing grapes and wine... Because of this versatility, the relatively small regions can live their own lives undisturbed.

The Hungarian tribes, ancestors of today's inhabitants, arrived at their present homeland precisely 1100 years ago from the Crimean peninsula. The Carpathian Basin was a favorite destination of nomads searching for pastures in the age of migration. However, since the Huns, Avars and other peoples continued to live in the social structure to which they had grown accustomed, they inevitably vanished. The Hungarians, however, arriving here in search of a more developed social structure, settled here and consciously integrated into the spirit of Christianity. Gerbert Aurillac, a statesman of genius, a great scientist of his age, the chancellor of the emperor of the Holy Roman Empire and later Pope Sylvester II for a short period, organized an effective buffer zone with admirable caution around what were then the borders of Christian Europe, out of the states of the newly settled warrior peoples. The Vikings or Normans strengthened into well-organized Christian states in Denmark, England and France's Normandy region, and along the Mediterranean Sea in the region of Sicily and the Kingdom of Naples. Sailing down from Sweden on the big rivers of what is now the Russian steppe, the Vikings – there called the Varegians – established the Russian state with Kiev as its seat. And Hungary completed the buffer zone constructed around Rome – leaving Byzantium with Greek rites – and also against the uninterrupted migratory waves rolling in from the direction of what is now Moldova. Thus the renewed migration attempts and the Ottoman/Turkish attacks were averted. Hungary was able to ensure peace not only by arms but also by a peaceful settlement policy. The Pechenegs, the Kuns and the Jazygians coming from the East were settled (their descendants still live in the Great Plains, in the "Kunság" and "Jászság"), as were the craftsmen of the war-plagued cities of the Netherlands, France and northern Italy, or the German industrialists and agriculturists engaged in forestry and mining.

King Stephen – who was crowned by the Pope, founded the Hungarian kingdom in the year 1000 and who was canonized in 1083 – organized a pilgrimage to the Holy Land.

"For one flying high above,

Poet Miklós Radnóti wrote about Hungary. For him this landscape was not a map but a homeland, just as it is for the author of this book, Péter Korniss, who shows the reader a desire to experience Hungary visually.

This guide embraces this small country with unconcealed emotion and affection. A picture always means an emotional identification, although one rarely speaks about it. The identification is as much for the photographer as for the viewer.

Painters also first experienced the landscape hiding behind the main subject – a range of hills, a row of trees waving in the background, the sketches of buildings. Then the landscape gradually gained ground and became a main subject. Sometimes a single branch or stunted tree conveys the image of a land or a country in the painter's soul.

Perhaps this has been true since the poet Francesco Petrarca climbed Mount Ventoux, the Hill of Winds near Avignon, on April 25, 1336, for no better reason than to enjoy the landscape spread before his eyes and to live it and learn it in a context never experienced from below. At the same time, he came closer to his own inner self by experiencing the view, as he himself wrote to his brother after the excursion. The shepherds and the people of the hill watched the hill-climbing fool and shook their heads – because only a fool would make the climb without the hope of any gain purely to see the view from there. It was a great moment, the birth of the Renaissance. "I was standing there stunned by the great spectacle, sort of going numb in the spell of the unusually light air," wrote Petrarca. There, on the summit, the poet took *The Confessions of St. Augustine* out of his pocket and flipping through the pages he read "People go to admire the high hills, the waves of the seas, the long, winding rivers and the tracks of the stars, but they hardly ever look into themselves." And then the poet understood that the depiction of one's landscape, environment, country and homeland can renew one's internal spiritual world.

This is how the relationship between the sight preserved in pictures and the viewer, conveyed by the creator and generating emotions and thoughts, came about.

It was as if the discovery and application of photography in the previous century had broken the spiritual relationship between the creator and his creation, as if the intention of purely conveying facts was intended to replace the artistic creative character. Distributing photographs of cities, villages, settlements and landscapes through postcards became a profitable business. Undoubtedly, in this way the people of far-flung continents were drawn closer together. The spectacle of a theater building, a beverage factory, a city hall, a railway station, a department store, a beach boardwalk or a local cable railway brought them into some shallow acquaintance. We recognized that we are all citizens of the same planet.

Naturally, these photographs were based on the principle of unconditional similarity, indicating that what the photographer recorded was what the viewer saw and was true and genuine. This kind of documentation, with its you-are-there immediacy, was coupled with the awakening of a sort of social civic self esteem and critical attitude (photos of war and of society).

There are, however, master photographers who attempt to capture in light the spectacle they wish to present so that it appears not as a subject in the inventory, nor as an attractive travel destination and not even as a document, but as the photographed section of the world selected in its spiritual reality. In its spiritual reality in the sense that a landscape, building or plant can also convey the metaphysical, spiritual essence of the experience provided by it – consider the trees of Altdorfer or van Gogh -- but primarily in the sense that, by his creation, the artist can provide a cathartic experience transcendentally valid and true beyond the direct reality and authenticity of the image.

Péter Korniss's pictures of Hungary bring to the viewer the soul of a country, the spiritual essence of a homeland. The affection towards the homeland is perceptible, but so is the joy of the discovered and created beauty. Discovered

The herons have taken wing from the Hortobágy reeds. Their tall legs, long bills and white wings move with timepiece perfection and ancient harmony. They start their flight with careless safety, without any excitement, still perhaps fleeing. The Hortobágy was preserved intact since the conquest of Hungary by the Magyars. Everything the ancient Hungarians appreciated was here: water, reeds, plains, grass, pastures and fish, birds, cattle and stud eager to

IN THE HORTOBÁGY NATIONAL PARK

WATER-WORLD IN SZATMÁR-BEREG

graze. Today, as a national park, the Hortobágy cherishes the precious but partly wasted remnants of the past like a living museum. Along the waters, the fertile decay offers shelter for thousands of tiny creatures. The picture with the fallen tree-trunk and the one-time boat – provided it is one – makes one feel that time and again wild floods will flow over everything to immerse the rich vegetation seen in the picture. The peaceful winter landscape with the frostbitten trees would depict an untouched world,

were it not for the fresh footprints visible in the snow.

The twin trees rising beside each other from the plowed land send a message to the Mátra hills looming in the distance, where lonely trees that have lost their way are rare in the dense forests. Or have they lost their way? Have they been planted? It used to be customary to plant cherry trees in the middle of the grain fields so that people tiring of working in the fields could pick their fruit. And the wife, arriving with a

lunch of bread and soup in a round basket on top of her head, just as the noon bell rang, could sit in the shadow of the tree and offer her husband lunch on the checkered tablecloth spread on the ground. Old military maps always included such lonely trees, so it never occurred to anyone to cut them. They were sacred living beings. But who bothers today to plant a cherry tree in the middle of the plowed land, kilometers from the village?

There are the white, red and yellow flowers, as if they were not industrial plants, although they are. As if their world of color were to captivate the eye consciously. The white flower bushes whisper the comforting proximity of a lake appearing faintly in the distance.

The innumerable shoal islands of the Danube may have taken their shape in order to inspire painters. The wedge-shaped island in the middle of the river, lying diagonally, forever posing a danger to sailors: would we see the first act of a drama that could occur any time? Most Hungarian painters settled in the Danube Bend precisely to see this sight.

A little almond tree blossoms proudly among the bare props of the Tokai vines; they seem useless now, because

LANDSCAPE

THE DANUBE EMBANKMENT IN WINTER

there are no vine posts yet providing support. It is widely known that the almond tree is the earliest blossoming tree; it daringly exposes itself to renewed attacks of winter cold.

The accompanying picture, a winter forest in the Bükk hills, with its geometric lines of bare trees, as if to justify Ernő Kállai's theory that even the most abstract work of art cannot surpass the abstractions of nature.

And now at last people and animals. Horses romping about in the corral in winter; three wise Lippizaner horses deep in thought discussing a theoretical problem. Then patches of grass, a flock of sheep starting out to the sun-drenched puszta, as the shepherd's dog, at his master's command, begins to bring order to the army entrusted to him.

Another dog disciplines a bull, quiet in the knowledge of his strength. This species of cattle, with shining gray hair and proud horns, has lived amidst the Hungarians for some 2000 years. Unfortunately, these cows are on the verge of extinction, because they are not as good milkers as the Swiss-German breed. However, their meat is tasty, they can be kept in the open all year round and are less susceptible to disease. The gray cattle approvingly acknowledges the shepherd caressing his dog as a prize for its successful cattle-driving skills.

And now the farmstead. The farmstead has already been mentioned in the introduction. Close to the road, it is still lonely. Defiant independence. Not even a TV antenna can be seen here. The famed nine-arch bridge of Hortobágy stretches over the Hortobágy River, where the gray cattle graze. The inn built at the bridgehead and the annual bridge fair are the notable meeting places for the shepherds from the neighborhood.

And now the hill with the crosses.

The Mongol attack that destroyed Óbuda was recalled in the introduction. In 1241 the Mongol light cavalry destroyed the Hungarian heavy armored army near the village of Muhi, on the bank of the Sajó River, with ease. An archbishop, a chancellor, bishops, princes and soldiers lost their lives there. The king barely managed to escape.

This battle is commemorated by a forest woven of wooden crosses; the bell is rung time and again by the wind in eternal remembrance of the victims who sacrificed themselves for their loved ones.

A backwater of the Danube River near Dunaföldvár

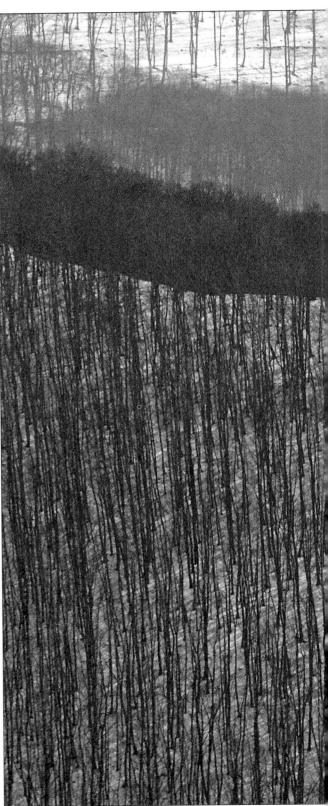

Spring in Tokaj / Winter in the Bükk

Lipizzaner stud in Szilvásvárad

A farmstead in the plains

The nine-arch bridge of Hortobágy

The memorial place of the Muhi battle

CASTLES

— SÜMEG CASTLE —

were, at the same time, the cradles of culture: thanks to Tamás Nádasdy, a printing shop was established in 1537 in Sárvár, where János Sylvester, later a university professor in Vienna, published a translation of the New Testament with the nobleman's financial support, and Sárospatak provided a home for the famous Reformed (Calvinist) college, still in operation.

The royal palaces differed from the private castles of the aristocrats both in their external appearance and function.

— SÁROSPATAK —

The first castles in the traditional sense, aside from royal seats and county centers, were built in the second half of the 13th century, following the Mongol invasion. These castles served not to guard the border but to enhance the protection and reputation of the owner. From the castle built onto the hill, distant areas could be seen and the work in the fields and merchants' trading could be supervised. The castle at Sümeg, west of Lake Balaton, aptly illustrates this. At the foot of the castle hill, the almost geometrically arranged settlement is visible where when the castle was still in use, people serving the big landowning aristocrats used to live: peasants, gardeners, craftsmen and merchants. The village and the its residents were essentially the property of the castle's master. The Csesznek castle was of similar nature among the forests of the Bakony hill, not far from Veszprém.

These castles in Transdanubia – like the Nagyvázsony castle of Pál Kinizsi, the commander – were built of stone. However, for the castles of the Great Plains, where stone was in short supply, brick was used for construction. Such is the Kisvárda castle in eastern Hungary, or rather its ruins, utilized today as a venue for theatrical performances. Kisvárda used to guard the border between the Transylvanian Principality and Habsburg-held northern Hungary; it frequently changed hands after fierce battles.

The castles of the Renaissance era provided more comfort for its dwellers, as is demonstrated by the Perényi palace in Sárospatak, beautified in the 16th century, or the Nádasdy palace of Sárvár in Transdanubia. The Perényi and Nádasdy families gave their homeland powerful statesmen in the 16th and 17th centuries. Both Sárospatak and Sárvár

A significant military force was also stationed in them. But these did not function as border fortresses either.

The Diósgyőr castle near Miskolc was a permanent residence of queens, and sometimes the kings resided here,

AND PALACES

for months, on their tours around the country.

The castle of Visegrád on the Danube Bend, in a position providing easy con-

—————— NAGYCENK ——————

trol over distant areas, was turned into the temporary capital by the Anjou kings of French origin, ruling in the 14th century. King Charles I, King Louis I and his daughter Queen Mary I governed the country from here; Visegrád was often the site of international summit meetings in the Middle Ages. Later, King Matthias Corvinus, who made Buda the country's capital again, built a holiday palace here. Tata, a settlement abundant in waters, was also a royal hunting castle where King Matthias liked to rest after a tiring day of hunting. The adornments of Renaissance taste on the Gothic window frames can be seen in the photo.

The fortress-like character of the oldest monasteries is an unusual feature. These monasteries were built and equipped to resist attacks. This protection was important not so much against foreign enemies but rather to protect the valuables safeguarded in the monastery.

The oldest monastery still operating in Hungary is the castle of Pannonhalma, inhabited by Benedictine monks. Under Saint Stephen's rule, the Benedictine order of monks, founded by Saint Benedict of Italy, cultivated sci-

—————— FERTŐD ——————

ences and also served the king in public administration. The arch-abbot of the monastery acts as a high priest, independent of the country's bishops and archbishops. The monastery of Pannonhalma was founded by King Saint Stephen around the year 1000 to honor Saint Martin – a guard officer in his youth and later the bishop of Tours, France – born in the Roman era in Savaria (today Szombat-

hely in Transdanubia or Pannonia). The king never launched a war without asking for the protection of Saint Martin. The Benedictine monastery, named after Saint Martin, gained the poetic name Pannonhalma only in the 19th century; before that it was called Saint Martin's Hill.

In the course of the 18th century, the nobility left their castles and moved to more comfortable palaces. Such is the palace of the great statesman and writer Count István Széchenyi in Nagycenk;

the palace of the Esterházy princes in Fertőd (called Esterháza until 1949) and the palace of the Festetics princes in Keszthely. Each of the palaces is surrounded by neatly planned parks, and magnificent music halls provide concert opportunities. The Eszterházy princes sponsored the composer Haydn. The Festetics family generously supported Hungarian literature.

The ruins of Csesznek Castle

The Visegrád Castle
with the Danube

The Nagyvázsony Castle

43

The adorned gate and richly
furnished rooms
of the palace of the Festetics
princes in Keszthely

Concert in the Festetics Palace

The ancient crypt
and Gothic cloister
of the Pannonhalma Abbey

The library of the abbey
with the sculpture of Saint Stephen

Section of the gala hall

The main gate
of the Fertőd Palace

THE VILLAGE

HORTOBÁGY

The apartments are separated from the court by a covered corridor-type space divided by columns. There is a well in the courtyard, covered by a wooden roof to protect it from bad weather. The houses were generally whitewashed; this was

FOLK HOUSE IN BARANYA

The Hungarian village is an agricultural community with family-owned single-story houses, huge gardens and hay fields in the plains; with enclosed gardens in the hilly areas and tiny flower gardens in front of the house. Every village had craftsmen but not of all trades. However, each of the villages kept smiths and boot-makers. The cooper, the barrel maker, was indispensable to vineyard areas. The church was usually built on a hill in the center of the village. As a separate settlement, a row of cellars stretched on the outskirts of the villages in fruit and vineyard areas, where the family moved to during vintage time or in the summer heat. A northern Hungarian village, Hollókő, hidden among hills and so preserved its ancient character untouched. It has been declared a protected area, a living museum. Similarly, a few dozen settlements of the Őrség in southwestern Hungary were preserved in their ancient state under the strict guardianship of forest-covered hills. As its name indicates, the Őrség was a region of guards: it was inhabited by soldiers' families who settled here in the Middle Ages to guard the borders. Since the area remained independent from counties and landlords, no castles, palaces or landlord's mansions were built here. The families lived independent lives, not compelled even to serve as serfs. The Őrség region spread to the areas that became part of Austria in 1920 (Burgenland), where some Hungarians still live today. The seat of the Austrian Őrség is Felsőőr (Oberwart). The picture of Szalafő presents a typical thatch-roofed dwelling in the Őrség. The thatched roof had long been in nationwide use and as it turned out, proved to be a useful, healthy, insulating yet ventilating type of roof. The house walls built of sun-dried clay bricks also proved effective. The picture taken in Nagytótfalu, Baranya County, presents the most characteristic building style in the country:

an effective method of preventing disease, since lime is a disinfectant. Yellowish whitewash – mixed with a kind of yellow clay – was rarer; it is visible on the house on Petőfi Street in Drávapalkonya.

The annual country fair, coupled with a bazaar, was a village festivity. Showmen set up their tents and the merry-go-round whirled. The day of the country fair was also the celebration of the village's patron saint. Every church and parish (where the births, christening ceremonies, weddings and deaths were registered) had a patron saint for whom some relic was hidden in the altar. On the patron saint's day, the population of the village (primarily in Catholic settlements; this habit is being abandoned in Calvinist villages) attended a mass, after which they swarmed out to the spacious area along the village border where marketers, honey-cake makers,

THE REFORMED CHURCH IN NAGYSZEKERES

furriers, meat roasters, boot-makers and potters lined up.

Generally, the churches are impressive buildings, maintained by the population and the priest with great care. If the church had no bell tower, an adjacent belfry was scaffolded. One example is the bell tower of Nagyszekeres in Szatmár in eastern Hungary. Here in Szatmár, then in Bereg and up in the Bodrogköz near the Tisza River, the conquering Hungarians who arrived from the Verecke pass first settled. These places have preserved the oldest traditions. For example, in the Szatmárcseke cemetery (the estate of the great Hungarian poet Ferenc Kölcsey, the author of the Hungarian national anthem), for a thousand years, without interruption, people erected tomb-posts carved in the shape of a boat, in remem-

HOLLÓKŐ

brance of the deceased who sailed to the other world on Charon's boat. The faithful village people erected a statue of the village's patron saint or most frequently, a statue of the Virgin Mary in the nearby fields along the roads.

In villages ruled by the landlord, the aristocrats – in competition with each other – built luxurious churches, equals of the most fashionable Western European, primarily French, styles of the time. The country is resplendent with such masterpieces, such as the Benedictine church of Ják. The church was consecrated by the Bishop of Győr in 1256. A smaller, movingly beautiful church is the one in Velemér. Its frescoes, impressive even in their shabbiness, tell sacred stories to the illiterate faithful coming in and looking around the church.

After the burden of workdays (mowing, animal tending, sheep watering) the villagers, wearing festive outfits, sometimes ancient folk costumes, celebrate the great holidays (such as Easter or Corpus Christi) by processions leading out into the countryside. One picture depicts the Easter festivities of Orthodox Gypsies in the village of Hodász in the Nyírség region. Birth, death, wedding and burial – festivities following the eternal cycle and rebirth of nature.

Among the Zala Hills

A typically Hungarian form of settlement:
a village in the Nyírség

Wine cellars in Palkonya

Modern architecture with an eye on the past in Nagykálló

Village street in the Bakony

The community house in Nagykálló

A peasant house in the Őrség

The Ják church

Hollókő, a village
of the World Heritage

Work in the fields

Grazing

Hoeing

Shepherd carving wood

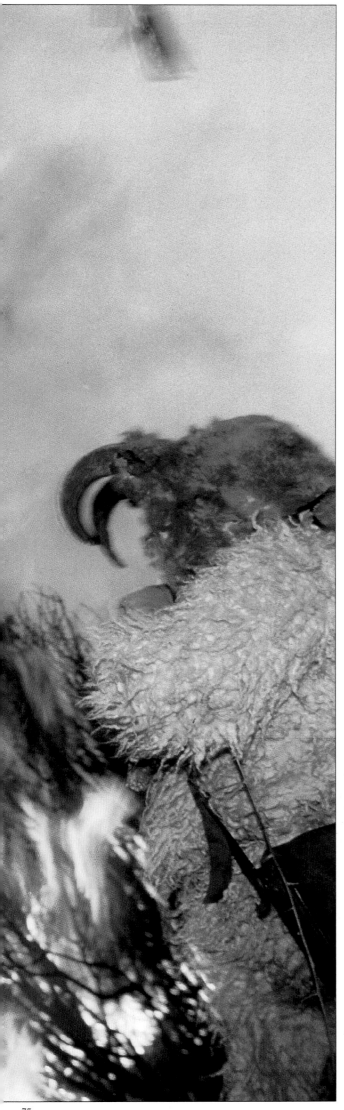

"Busó" procession in Mohács

Easter procession in Hollókő

Easter open-air mass in Hodász

The Lord's Day procession
in Rimóc
of those taking their
First Communion

In the fair

In the Rimóc Church

The Szatmárcseke Cemetery

DEBRECEN

development of the past 50 years altered the old townscape and the big housing estates changed the town's character. Pécs, Esztergom and Eger however, preserved their ancient appearance. Pécs is unusual in that while the monumental cathedral with four towers is situated in the middle of a beautiful park, a few hundred meters away on the main square, a Turkish mosque has been transformed into a Catholic church, its ancient architectural features preserved. Of the episcopal towns however, Eger cherishes the ornate taste of the enlightened 18th century: the victory of modern sciences has been immortalized in Sigrit's frescoes, painted at the end of the 18th century in the episcopal school and library. Eger Castle, once an episcopal castle-fortress and cathedral, today attracts thousands of visitors with the relics of the fortress system. This castle, far from any

The towns of Hungary – with the exception of episcopal, principal and county seats – developed in the 13th century. The bourgeoisie became rich and organized into a political force in the 14th century. From then on, kings accepted them as their allies against the nobles and they received free royal town titles. Nobles were not even allowed to move into a free royal town without permission.

In design, administration and appearance, the towns of Transdanubia and northern Hungary rival Western European towns. Some Transdanubian towns are of Roman origin, such as Óbuda (Aquincum), Pécs (Sopianae) and Szombathely (Savaria). One photo in this album depicts the stone road of Szombathely built by the Romans about 1600 years ago.

The centers and main attractions of the towns are their main squares. Churches are also important, but these were centrally

SÁROSPATAK

placed only in episcopal towns (Esztergom, Pécs and Eger). The episcopal church and castle of Veszprém, built on a hill, is also centrally positioned but the

border, was besieged in 1552 by the Turkish sultan's huge army, but the few thousand defenders resisted successfully. In memory of this victory, Eger has become

THE TOWN

———— SZOMBATHELY ————

ic church and fin-de-siècle architecture stand near the sculpture of Lajos Kossuth, the hero of the War of Independence.

It is intriguing how self-consciously the small towns follow the latest architectural trends. Paks and Siófok asked Imre Makovecz to build their churches; these buildings are masterpieces of organic architectural style. A housing complex in Sárospatak, decorative in spite of its affectation, is characteristically up-to-date.

The towns of the plains developed dif-

building in a spread-out village pattern. This is how these cities grew big. Otherwise, Kecskemét, for example, became prosperous through major exports of cattle, and huge pastures were required for animal husbandry (Bugac). Debrecen developed similarly, the only difference being that the town never came under direct Turkish rule. Thus its cultural institutions (a college, a printing house) were also more developed. Kecskemét outdoes itself with the colorful, turn-of-the-centu-

———— MISKOLC ————

the symbol of successful military and national resistance.

Of the burgher's towns of Transdanubia, Pécs, Kőszeg and Sopron managed to preserve their old townscape the most, although Sopron was hit by devastating air strikes in the early summer of 1945, as was Szombathely, where only traces of the old town are visible. Tiny Kőszeg however, with its town hall adorned with a coat-of-arms and a Madonna, and its unexpectedly turning and winding streets – to cause the enemy to lose his way in them – gives the impression of a movie set.

For decades Miskolc, in northern Hungary, was the second largest town in the country. Its architecture is interesting in that its housing estates, built one after the other, and its hasty construction projects at the beginning of the century remind one of American towns. However, a Goth-

ferently from cities in western Hungary. Debrecen, Szeged and Kecskemét are major peasant towns. Kecskemét and Szeged were ruled by the Turkish sultan for one-and-a-half centuries. The dwellers of the tiny villages fled to the towns for safety and swelled them by following their traditional architectural style,

ry facades in the Hungarian Secessionist style, while Szeged gained its present form through a votive church, a square around it and the university building complex built after a catastrophic flood in the past century. Open-air theater performances are held on the square in front of the cathedral every summer.

Medieval houses in Sopron

A street in Sopron

The medieval main square in Sopron

In downtown Székesfehérvár

Eger Castle: the legendary site
of the fight against the Turks

Franc
pinxit

igrist.
1781.

The fresco in the Lyceum's library

Justitia's sculpture in downtown Eger

Mass in the Esztergom Basilica

Szentendre moments

The
Evangelical
Church
in Siófok:
a master-
piece
of organic
architecture

The Pécs Cathedral with the castle wall

Street section with a fountain in Pécs

The Cifra Palace in Kecskemét

A church section in Paks

Storno House
in Sopron

The chapel
of Esztergom
Castle

The facade
of the Szeged
Cathedral

A Baroque street
section in Eger

The Balaton, Hungary's largest lake, has been a preferred holiday resort since ancient times. Even today the remnants of Roman villas accompany it. The Balaton is an attractive lake not only for its excellent climate and the beautiful region surrounding it, but also because of its origins. Geysers that sprang up in the wake of volcanic outbreaks in the Balaton's north shore and the large volume of rain at the time filled up a shell-shaped dip that became the Lake Balaton of today. The lake therefore, is not the remnant of a prehistoric sea. As a result the water has a pleasant velvetiness, and curative waters abound in the neighborhood (like Hévíz and Balatonfüred). The Balaton's shallow water warms up quickly. At 600 square kilometers, the Balaton's area is larger than that of Lake Geneva. Even so, the Balaton contains only one-fiftieth as much water as Lake Geneva. For this reason the sudden storms are extremely dangerous, because they lash

THE FORTRESS CHURCH IN VÖRÖSBERÉNY

up the shallow water into unusually high waves.

Lake Balaton once spread over almost half of Transdanubia; it was the Romans who began to regulate it, driving off some of its water through the predecessor of today's Sió channel. Tihany, Badacsony, Szigliget and some other hills were islands in the Middle Ages. Unfortunately, the abundant fish population – the pike-perch, for example – and some species of birds are headed for extinction.

Lake Balaton is a favorite topic of poems, plays, novels and short stories. And paintings of the lake could fill an entire gallery. It is natural, then, that the Balaton continues to pose new challenges for the photographer as well.

It would be unreasonable to explain the visual wonders of the lake and its surroundings, because the artist's photographs speak for themselves. So here let's only refer to the pictures of the sailboats sailing, the spectacle of the sun-

LAKE BALATON

A PEASANT BAROQUE WINE-PRESS
HOUSE ON SZENT GYÖRGY HILL

Balaton in wintertime, the splendor of twilight, the wine-press houses tucked comfortably among the fruit trees of the Balaton's north shore and the shots immortalizing the winter magic of Szigliget in an almost Brueghel-like atmosphere. And to certify that photography also has a humorous side, look at the amusing picture showing holidaymakers crouched behind the window-eyes of a luxury hotel as prisoners of sunshine.

A few explanatory words are needed for the photo of the Tihany peninsula. This range of hills bordered by water, with the exception of a narrow strip of land, with an internal lake in the middle of the peninsula – as seen in the picture – safeguards important moments in Hungarian history and culture. Following the example of King Stephen, the founder of Pannonhalma, Stephen's successor King Andrew, established a Benedictine monastery here which, although transformed, still exists today. The doc-

ument establishing this monastery in the 1050s includes the oldest surviving written words of Hungarian. King Andrew is buried in the same monastery: his tomb in the crypt is covered by a simple marble plate adorned with cross-shaped swords.

It is interesting, however, that no noble families settled around the shores of the lake; there are no major castles. Aristocrats maintained smaller holiday houses, if at all. The only aristocratic family of the Balaton area, the Festetics princes - mentioned in the chapter on castles - built their Keszthely palace in such a splendid manner, supporting Hungarian culture in every respect, because Emperor Joseph II sent into exile the Festetics family member who demanded that Hungarian hussars be permitted to use their mother tongue in the army.

However, the Balaton environment is all the more rich in the picturesque mansions of the cultured lesser nobility.

shine changing by the time of day (or even by the hour) sending reflections on the water, the attraction of ice on Lake

Seagulls above the lake

Play   A hotel on the Aranypart
                                          (Golden Shore)

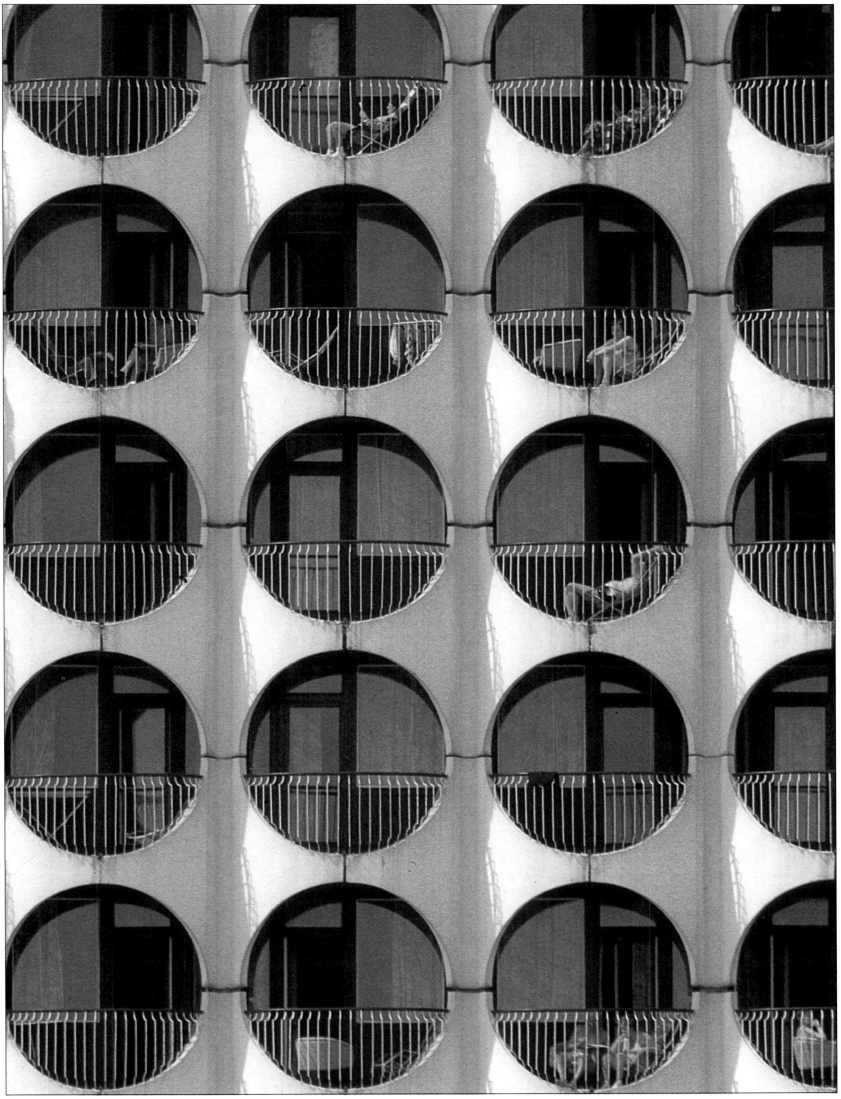

The Tihany peninsula
with the inner lake

Szigliget in winter

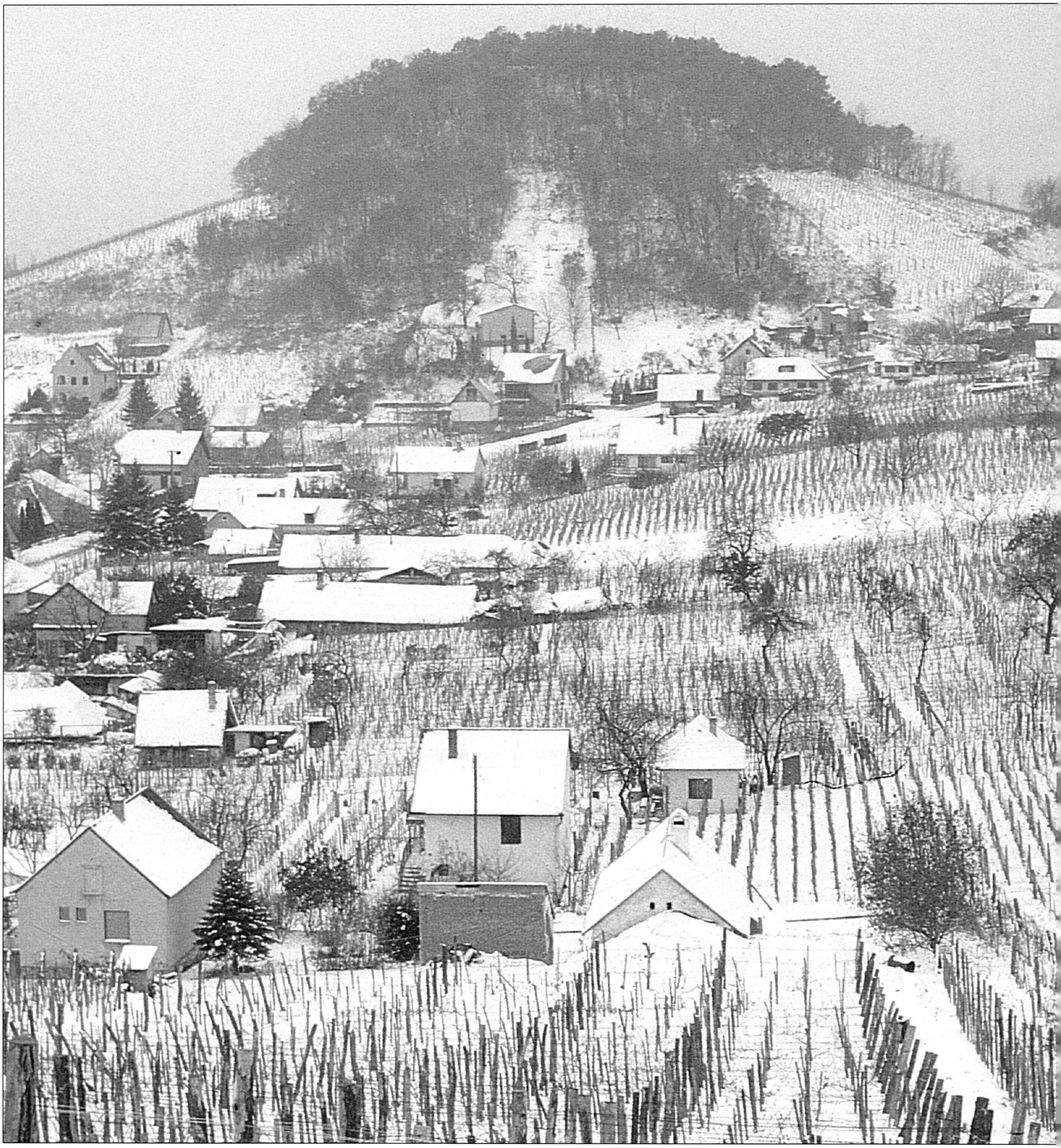

Vine garden in spring

The lake at Örvényes

The ice-covered Füred bay

Sailboats taking a rest
at Balatonalmádi

BUDAPEST

Whoever travels to the Hungarian capital for the first time can observe the settlement styles of many centuries and the geographical circumstances that shaped Budapest. An outpost of the Roman Empire was situated here on the banks of the Danube; it was protected by a fortress somewhere at what is now the Pest bridgehead of the Elizabeth Bridge. This fortress was later surrounded by the town of Pest. On the other bank of the Danube, in the neighborhood of today's Árpád Bridge, to replace the Roman city of Aquincum, medieval Buda was established; however, it was destroyed by the 1241 Mongol attack. Then King Béla IV moved Buda to its present place, a rocky-

VÁCI STREET

AQUINCUM

carstic hill rising above the Danube River. (The old city got the name Óbuda and has been called that ever since.) A carefully planned town was built here in the 1250s. After its heyday in the Renaissance era, the town and Buda Castle itself came

under Turkish rule for one-and-a-half centuries, and the united European armed forces managed to reclaim it only in 1686. The 150-year Turkish occupation destroyed much of what had been created in the Renaissance era. The Turkish relics however, lend the city a special color. Buda served as the capital of the country several times but not without interruptions. Pest, Buda and Óbuda merged as Budapest, the country's current capital, in the last third of the past century. Óbuda remained a village-like settlement for a long time, Buda preserved its medieval character, while Pest developed rapidly.

Its Secessionist buildings are significant both in number and artistic value.

The siege of Budapest in the winter of 1944-1945 caused dreadful devastation. A number of photographers and painters lived off the horrifying pictures of this event for decades. Budapest was the only European capital at the end of World War II to be destroyed in house-to-house fighting. With the exception of Warsaw, which had suffered since the autumn of 1939, Bucharest, Sofia, Belgrade, Zagreb, Ljubljana, Bratislava and Prague remained almost intact. Rome managed to declare itself an open city. Although Hitler ordered

——— BUDA CASTLE ———

Since 1945 Pest has been the center of government, public administration, industry, trade and finance. The Buda Royal Palace houses a museum center today; parks here still safeguard the tombstones with the turban from the era of Turkish occupation. The Parliament building on the Pest embankment of the Danube, a grandiose Neo-Gothic palace, was the legislative center of a state still significant before 1918. In the much smaller country of today, the Parliament can now house the prime minister's and the head of state's offices in addition to the legislative body.

By its versatility in layout, this city of two million enables the artist to share the joy of discovery with the reader, not in the manner of pictorial guidebooks, but to "build up" his own Budapest from the harmonies or, more accurately, the disharmonies of colors, forms, lights and shadows.

One can imagine the two towers of a church in the Vizíváros district of Buda keeping a guard's eye on the new town section with its monotonous housing estates behind Margaret Bridge. The row of windows of the Hotel Hilton, built on the foundations of a medieval Dominican monastery, the Fisherman's Bastion, a church on the Danube bank and a church ruin with a triple tower complex in the Castle District exchange messages. But the proudest tower, this lattice-work building, the tower of the Our Lady Cathedral, popularly known as Matthias Church, rules self-consciously over this section of the city, on the main square where the single-story, tiny-looking building once used to serve as the Buda town hall.

The commander taking a proud glance from his anxious horse onto the Danube; the ancient totem, the turul bird, spreading its wings beside the one-time palace restored from the ruins; the cross beneath

——— A TURKISH TOMB ———

Paris set ablaze, the German military commanders spared it. They acted similarly in the capitals of Belgium, the Netherlands, Denmark and Norway. Still, one fortunate result emerged from this horror. After Buda Castle and the Castle District were almost totally razed, the buried medieval palace, buildings and treasures were unearthed. After modernization, the medieval houses were made habitable again. Perhaps even in Rome not as many people, ordinaly families, live in original medieval houses as in Buda. The pictures of these streets, houses, squares and churches evince the people's will to endure.

the Gothic arches of the royal chapel warning like an exclamation point: these are more than photographs, these are visions provoking thoughts and emotions.

The towers of the Saint Anne Church, the Danube River
and the Margaret Bridge in the background

The Hotel Hilton, the Fisherman's Bastion
and the church on Szilágyi Dezső Square

Baroque castle gate,
with statue of Eugene of Savoy
(on horseback) in the background

The palace in Buda Castle, housing the National Gallery

Matthias Church

The medieval castle chapel

A courtyard in Dísz Square

Snow-covered courtyard
in Fortuna Street

Winter on Margaret Island

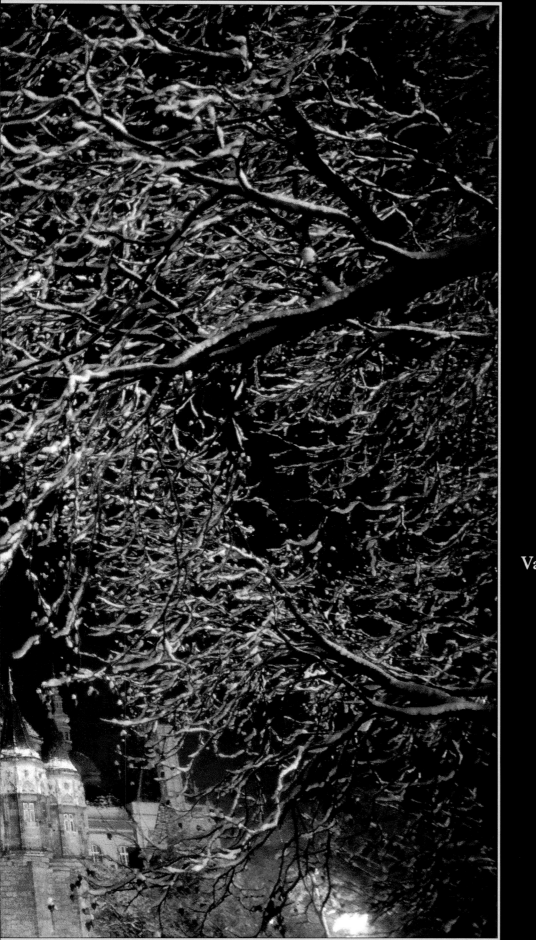

Vajdahunyad Castle in Városliget

The well of the Nereids
on Ferenciek Square

An ornament adorning
a Neo-Renaissance apartment
house on Andrássy Avenue

The sculptures of the Basilica

The Dohány Street Synagogue

A masterpiece of Hungarian Secessionism:
the Museum of Applied Arts

A balcony in the Józsefváros District

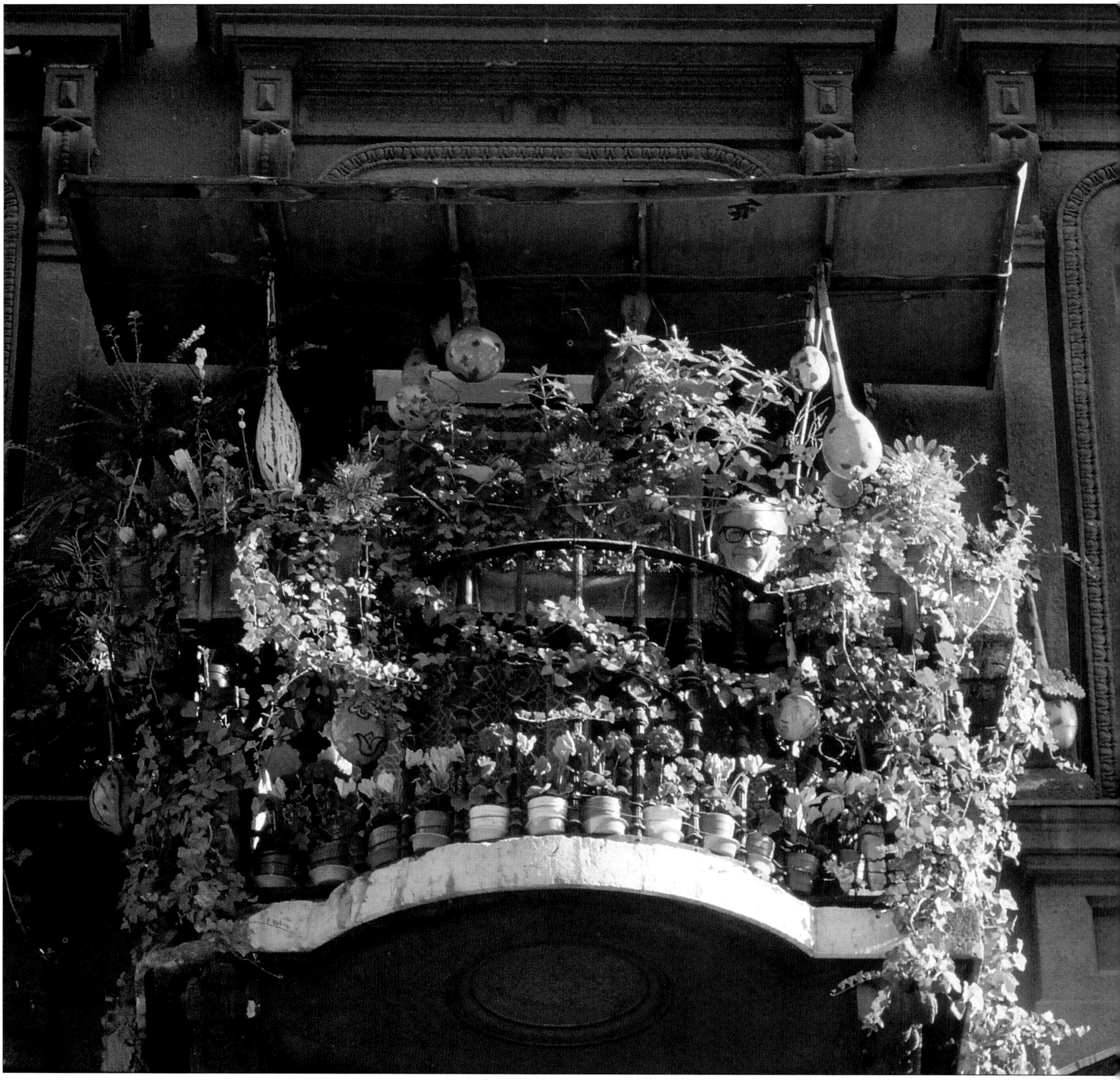

Graduation celebration

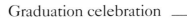

The New York Café

A turn-of-the-century carousel
in the Városliget

The Saint Stephen Boulevard in late afternoon

Heroes' Square

DESIGNER: JULIANNA RÁCZ / 9S MŰHELY

TRANSLATED BY GABRIELLA SCHÖN

LANGUAGE EDITOR: CHRIS SPRINGER

COPYRIGHT

© PÉTER KORNISS, 1996 – PHOTOS

© ISTVÁN NEMESKÜRTY – TEXT

INITIATED BY THE KREATÍV MÉDIA WORKSHOP

PRODUCER: JÓZSEF BÖJTE

OFFICINA NOVA, 1996

PUBLISHER: DR. BALÁZS KRATOCHWILL

TYPESETTING BY 9S MŰHELY

PRINTING BY KOSSUTH PRINTING HOUSE

ISBN 963 548 379 1